Rapunzel's Parrot

Rapunzel's Parrot

Jerry Bradley

Copyright © 2022 Jerry Bradley
All Rights Reserved

ISBN: 978-0-9987364-5-7
Library of Congress Control Number: 2021950071
Manufactured in the United States

Angelina River Press
Fort Worth, Texas

Acknowledgments

The author gratefully acknowledges the following publications where versions of these poems previously appeared:

Iron Horse Literary Review
    "We Were Warned"

I-70 Review
    "Three Travelers"

The New English Verse
    "The Haunted House"

Inheritance of Light: Contemporary Poetry (Denton, TX: University of North Texas Press, 1996)
    "Fairy Tale"

The World Retold
    "The Frog King"

Writing Texas
    "The Dead Son"
    "Donkey, Dog, Cat, and Ram"
    "In the Company of Mice"
    "Kind of Heart, Fair of Face"
    "The King's Twelve Daughters"
    "The Ogre at Breakfast"
    "The Ox-Cart Driver's Lament"
    "The Princess's Riddle"
    "The Test"
    "Today I Bake, Tomorrow I Brew"
    "The Transvestite Wolf"
    "The Youngest Daughter"

CONTENTS

Poems

11	In the Company of Mice
12	Today I Bake, Tomorrow I Brew
14	We Were Warned
15	The King's Twelve Daughters
17	The Transvestite Wolf
18	The Dead Son
19	A Bungled Chore
21	Kind of Heart, Fair of Face
23	The Haunted House
24	The Poor Man and the Devil
27	A Lesson for the Wolf
28	The Queen and the Jester
29	The Old Woman's Wish
30	Bleat, Little Goat
32	The Ox-Driver's Lament
33	The Princess's Riddle
35	The Ogre at Breakfast
36	The Two Brothers
38	Beauty and the Beast
39	Three Sluggards
41	The Frog King
42	The Little Tailor and the Flies
43	The Boy Who Wanted To Learn What Fear Was
44	A Better Bargain
47	Three Bears
48	The Youngest Daughter
49	Until the Leaves Tremble
51	Puss 'n Boots
53	The Farmer's Chickens
54	The Shoemaker
55	Today Given, Tomorrow Sold
57	Thumb
58	On the Other Hand
59	The Giant Killer
60	The Hatchlings
63	Prince Charming Breaks His Silence
64	The Test
65	Three Fables, One Moral
67	A Rose by Another Name

68	Little Brother
70	Turnips Below Ground, Corn Above
71	Three Travelers
72	The Prince's Wingmen
75	One Father's Trick
77	Fairy Tale
78	A Game of Chicken
79	Donkey, Dog, Cat, and Ram

Illustrations

10	"Cinderella" by Lois Lensky
16	"Little Red Riding Hood" by Arthur Rackham
20	"Snow White" by Warwick Goble
26	"The wolf and the seven young kids" by Heinrich Leutemann or Carl Offterdinger
34	"The boy who was never afraid" by John Bauer
40	"Greeting the Frog" by Walter Crane
46	"The Three Bears" by Arthur Rackham
50	"Puss in Boots" in *Fairy Tales that Never Grow Old*
52	"Chicken Little" by J. G. Chandler
56	"The Spider and the Fly" by Arthur Rackham
62	"Sleeping Beauty" by C.M. Burd

"Cinderella" by Lois Lensky in *Fairy Tales that Never Grow Old*, 1923.

In the Company of Mice

Cinderella slept in ashes near the oven
worn out as a hound
eating crow today, soup the next,
at last the red-combed rooster

whose wishbone she kept
wrapped in cloth
in her apron pocket

each night beneath the kettle
she looked for lentils in the soot
and prayed to her dead mother

oh when, oh when will he come?
she wondered
dreaming of rich gowns

even when her shoes
were worn out from dancing alone
she bided her time

waiting for the hansom coach,
a magic wand, and two loaves of bread,
for doves to peck out her step-sisters' eyes

Today I Bake, Tomorrow I Brew

A drunken miller lies to the king,
"See how the sun strikes my daughter's hair!
She can spin straw into gold."

But fathers always exaggerate
the beauty of their daughters,
and the next day, as days do, things get worse.
In the tower she can't do it; however, an imp can,
so she pays him with a necklace and a ring.

Next days often go like the first,
but on the crucial third she is out of jewels.
(Some women say this tale proves that baubles
are always a splendid gift.). Still he converts
the straw on the promise of her first-born.

She regrets the bargain, but Rumpelstiltskin wants
a kid, especially since he's too ugly to get one of his own.
The girl cries and cries, but he turns away from her
like Miles Davis at Carnegie Hall.
I'll give him back, he says, *if you can guess my name.*
Who's your daddy, who's your daddy? he intones.
Then he volunteers all sorts of misleading clues.

Months pass, and she grows rounder than a vintner's cask.
And each day she guesses new names:
Reginald? Theodore? Siegfried? Aloysius?

Later the mother of ravens overhears him
gloating in the forest. He's prancing about
like Mick Jagger in "Sympathy for the Devil"
gliding across lichen and ferns,
an evil Nijinsky before his time. Then he stamps
his foot so hard that it goes into the ground
and he can't break free. He struggles and strains
until the soles of his shoes bleed. He tears his meniscus
before ripping himself entirely in two. His sack of pearls scatters.

The miller happens by and scoops up the gems.
With them he returns to the alehouse and buys a round,
then another, then a goose with feathers of pure gold.

We Were Warned

we read the tales expecting the necessaries
we've always wanted:
morals and nixies and water-dwelling trolls

the voice like Rapunzel's parrot
ready to tell us all it knows

calling to the glass mountains
where dwarfs sledge ores
and evil queens dance on firecoals

they sing of the destroyed cottage
where the bears lived,
the big bad wolf with his belly full of stones,

but when at last we read them again,
we have become the wronged orphans
and are as lost as misaddressed mail

we collect mosses for our bed
and haul sacks of grain to the mill

I have learned to live
under the power of curses,
a changeling child
who once chased pearls

not this shaking donkey
shambling his way to the knacker

The King's Twelve Daughters

The king's twelve daughters slept
in beds side by side in a locked room.
But every morning when he unlatched the door,
he saw that the shoes of each had holes
in their soles.	He worried that they had been meeting
secret lovers at night, dancing with unsavory men
who might ruin their reputations.	So he chose
an ugly squire to watch them and placed his bed
amid theirs. That night the eldest brought the squire
a cup of wine, and they drank until his eyelids
were heavy and he began to snore.	With that
the whole dozen rose, opened wardrobes and cupboards,
and put on pretty dresses. Then they twirled with one another
until their shoes were worn to pieces.	At last
they too slept, though each dreamed the squire
was her own hedgehog lover, a man on whom she could walk
but who would then pierce her repeatedly until she bled.

"Little Red Riding Hood" by Arthur Rackham in *Fairy Tales of the Brothers Grimm*, 1909.

The Transvestite Wolf

to soften his voice he swallowed chalk
then washed himself in milk
and donned Grandma's paper frock

outside, the sparrows chattered together
tried to warn the old woman's scullion
granddaughter when she arrived

but the wolf's appetite was already
churning faster than a duck
in gutterwater

children smell like sausages to a wolf
so there'd be no more yarn rinsing
for that girl

oh, one day the ferryman
would likely carry the beast
to the underworld for his deed

but you know he'd be jumping
on the deck all the way
just like a sailor at a gay wedding

The Dead Son

after the child died
    he appeared at night
wearing the white shroud
    he wore into his coffin

his mother saw him
    in those places where
now beyond sleep and hunger
    he'd sat and played

a wreath of flowers
    'round his head
his soul as light
    as a bird or bread

poor boy who'd never
    had the chance
to slash raindrops with a sword
    or learn to dance

A Bungled Chore

The king's son was ambitious and wanted to usurp
the old man's throne, but the old fellow was wiser.
He summoned the lad and spoke of retirement.
"I will surrender the crown when you bring me
 the prettiest little dog in the kingdom to amuse me
when I withdraw from public life."
                                    The young lad
set off to do just that, but he was overtaken
by a violent storm from which he took refuge
in a nearby palace. There he heard sweet voices singing
and discovered a magnificent dining room with a table
set for two. Then a small figure came in
keening mournfully.
                       The figure – a very fine white cat –
removed her veil and greeted the prince. Then they dined
upon a sumptuous meal, and at bedtime she led him
to an elegant chamber. The next morning he awakened
to the sound of five hundred cats wailing outside his window.

"Snow White" by Warwick Goble in *The Fairy Boo*, 1913.

Kind of Heart, Fair of Face

I.

Snow White slept unhappily in a ray of light,
Monday's child, a poisoned comb in her hand,
her glass coffin as snug as a chaffinch's nest.
Magnificent pears hung from the branches above.

The huntsman told to kill her spared her,
slew instead a boar in the cold northland
and carried its lungs and liver in his vest
to her wicked step-mother who ate them with cloves.

Without housekeeper and incapable of preparing a single bite,
that woman ate whatever was at hand;
she seemed to like hearts and gizzards best
although I've heard she was also fond of turtledove.

Young Snow slept that way much of her life
until a traveling prince saw her empty left hand
and was stunned. He put his own over her breast
and swore what he knew about undying love.

We like it when stories end right
and no one follows the queen's command.
But be careful about what you ingest,
and always handle step-children with a kid's glove.

II.

Afterward the old lady danced and danced until she dropped
and sank with her iron slippers into the moat;
then Snow's thoughts turned again to the diamond mine.
She refused to sweep or clean and plopped
onto the dwarfs' settee where she napped for years in peace,
a bon-bon and a piece of poison apple still in her throat.

III.

What's worse than contaminated fruit?
Old Cronos devoured his own children,

Fearing that a little bird might
Throw a golden chain around its father's neck.

Bluebeard hanged his wives
By their hair in a dark closet.

Heed the premonitions, but like a fool
Wage war against heaven.

Some of you will not remember
Every word I say:

How some women will do anything
To get out of housework.

They sleep with a cross under their pillow,
Think all fairy tales end in gold.

The Haunted House

The haunted house always keeps its lights on.
It is where the woman who resembles your mother
Sits and mends. *Welcome,* she says. *Come in.*

What kind of man could resist? It is the place
He goes when he's tired of not fitting in.
Welcome, she says. *Look at what the wind blew in.*

But the bedrooms are empty now,
And it's too late to worry about ghosts or the weather,
As pointless as trying to sew eggs back together.

He knows what happened here,
Knows where everyone has gone.
The haunted house always keeps its lights on.

The Poor Man and the Devil

The poor man kept his promise to sit beside the grave
of his neighbor. And when the devil came at midnight
for the old man's soul, the poor man would not yield.
He had seen hard times and was not cowed.

Then the demon offered to bribe the fellow
with a bag of money if he'd go back home.
One bag won't do, he replied. I need enough gold
to fill my boot. So the devil sped to town

to speak to the moneychanger. Meanwhile, the poor man
took his knife and opened the sole of the boot.
When the devil returned with a bag of gold,
he poured it in, but the boot would not fill.

Go back and bring more! the poor man ordered,
and the dark one did. He brought an even larger bag,
and the gold clinked loudly as it fell, but the bargain
came to nothing because the boot could not be filled.

On his third trip the devil labored under the weight
on his shoulder. Still he could not top the poor man's boot.
And as the sun began to rise, the devil was forced to flee.
Sunrays filled his footprints, and fiery coals bit at his heels.

Smiling as bright as a mirror, the poor man
scooped up his boot and headed to town,
but along the way he was beset and killed
by a robber whose heart was hard and pitiless.

As a boy I was forced to drag my sledge
into the forest to fetch wood, but I had no trade.
All I owned was my knapsack, an old shooting coat,
and riding boots that would not fill.

Only in old age when they were
laid beside my grave
next to me in the tall grass
were my duties discharged.

"The wolf and the seven young kids" by Heinrich Leutemann or Carl Offterdinger in *Mein erstes Märchenbuch,* c1890.

A Lesson for the Wolf

When the wolf gave birth, she invited
a relative to be godfather, the fox
who was clever and could instruct her son
and help him forward in the world.

It is our duty he said *to take care
of this pup. I know a sheepfold
from which we might fetch him a scrap.*
Then he pointed far away.

*You will be able to creep in
without being seen while
I go to the other side to learn
if I can filch a pullet or hen.*

Once inside, the wolf was busier
than a broommaker as she chased
lambs around the pen. Finally
the old ram butted her down.

As she limped away, she saw
the fox near the farmhouse
beside a bowl of cat food
where he had lain down to rest.

Though neither had a penny
for a biscuit, the fox
never suffered for his trouble:
that was a lesson worth chewing on.

The Queen and the Jester

The queen and the jester kissed
until they were both puffing
like pigs on an exercycle.

But even a stone-built castle
may not offer a strong foundation
for forbidden love.

So they kissed again and then again
until in time they were at last ready
to blow their straw house down.

The Old Woman's Wish

Pressed by age and infirmity, an old beggar
came to a house and asked alms from a smith
who offered to cure his torments so that
the beggar would be able to earn his own bread.

He put on coals and blew the bellows,
and, when the fire sparked large and high,
the smith pushed him into the flames
until he glowed like the rose of paradise.

Then he tossed him into the quenching tub.
The water cooled the beggar as it closed him over,
and the man sprang out fresh and straight
and young. And when the smith's mother

asked if the fire had burnt him much,
he answered that he felt as if he had sat in dew.
The words landed on the old woman's ears like angels' breath,
and early the next morning she asked her son

to make her young again too, a bounding girl of eighteen.
So the smith stoked his fire and thrust her in:
she writhed this way and that, uttered terrible cries,
and grew hotter than a chiltepin.

When her rags were singed, he took her out
and threw her into the cooling tub, but she did not mend,
all because old people get angry with age the way sleepwalkers
do with the night, the way open doors do with the wind.

Bleat, Little Goat

I am the mouse who drove the coach
bleat, little goat, bleat

I am the hare that ate the cabbage leaf
bleat, little goat, bleat

I am the roe that grazed at her side
the stag that leapt merrily by

I go as the feathers fly
bleat, little goat, bleat

I am the bear that ate the berries
cry, little dove, cry

I stood over her bed with watchful fairies
cry, little dove, cry

when mishap overtook us
I could no longer sing

I failed her from my perch above
my head beneath my wing

I was the one who jumped the wave
swim, little fish, swim

I am the eagle that ate the trout
swim, little fish, swim

I polished the bolt and pushed it back
I let the prince come in and out

I have the hook still in my mouth
swim, little fish, swim

I rose at dawn and stood by the bed
weep, little child, weep

I made a fire and stroked her head
weep, little child, weep

I poured the tea from a kettle of brass
never again to hear her laugh

I poured the tea into my lap
weep, little child, weep

The Ox-Cart Driver's Lament

The king rode atop his golden saddle
until robbers fell upon him
and hanged him from a tree.

The ox that pulls his body now
once hauled turnips. I drive that cart,
but no man envies me

Though I understand the stars,
the tracks of the winds,
the desert sands, and the sea.

I am the bird who sharpens
his beak upon a diamond,
but wealth means nothing to me.

The Princess's Riddle

I have two kinds of hair on my head.
What color are they, cook?

They must be black and white
like pepper and salt.

Wrongly guessed;
let the tailor answer.

If not black and white, then brown
and red, like my father's Sunday coat.

Wrongly guessed;
let the fisherman speak.

The princess has silver and
gold on her head.

Soon the whole town knew
she was pouring coffee

into his saucer. The bright lad brought
her to life, just like the sun had her hair.

"The boy who was never afraid" by John Bauer in *En Konstnär Och Hans Sagovärld*, 1912.

The Ogre at Breakfast

Sunk in the weary dismals
beyond the drop edge of yonder,
he stares at his dish.

Appetite is his clock:
the big hand always telling him
when to move on.

The eggs he savors look like twins,
but they're not even cousins.
He keeps weasels in the woodshed

in case he cannot recall
his last meal. And what smells better
than happiness on the grill?

Salads are off menu; dinner always walks
with a limp. He rubs his hands, bares his teeth,
smiles like the duck that swallowed the queen's ring.

The Two Brothers

A boar laid waste to a farmer's field and killed his cattle.
When the lamentations reached the king, he offered
his daughter's hand to reward whoever
would capture or kill it. Two brothers, sons of a poor man,
undertook the hazard. And to find the beast,
they entered the woods from opposite sides.
When the younger had gone a short way,
a small man with a spear stepped up to him.
I give you this because your heart is pure and good.
Hold this, and the boar will do you no harm.

Before long the beast rushed at him in such fury
that it ran right into the spear and its heart was broken.
The lad then dragged the monster behind him
as he went homeward to the king.

At the other side of the thicket stood an alehouse
where people were making merry with wine and dance.
His elder brother had gone there to drink down some bravery,
but, when he saw his brother emerge with the carcass,
his heart gave him no peace. He called out
for his brother to come in and refresh himself.

The brothers drank there until evening. Then in darkness
they came to a bridge. The elder let the other go first,
and, when they were half-way across, he gave him a blow
from behind, knocking him dead. He buried him
beneath the bridge and carried the boar to the king.

But nothing stays hidden forever, and black deeds
always come to light. Years later a shepherd
driving his herd saw a white bone in the sand.
He thought it would make a good mouthpiece for his horn,
and, when he blew through it, the bone began to sing.

Even a bad coroner knows every body has stories to tell.
Though he'd married the girl, the wicked brother was sewn up in a sack
and drowned. You may think you'll end up in a beautiful tomb,
but don't count on your old bones or family skeletons
to give your old heart much rest.

Beauty and the Beast

A rich merchant had three daughters, all of them gorgeous,
Especially the youngest whom everyone called Beauty.
But when the merchant lost his fortune in the Bitcoin collapse,
He lost most of his property except for a small cottage
Where he tilled the lavender fields; as he did, Beauty looked after
The house while her sisters lay in bed reading screen magazines
And grumbling about their lost wealth.

When the merchant heard that a semi containing
Overdue goods was on its way, the family was excited.
He met the truck at the loading dock to receive the cargo,
But his creditors were there too, and he returned home
As poor as when he'd left. He ached to remember the fine suits
He once wore, how he once admired himself in the looking glass.

We know how the story goes. To save her father,
Beauty shacked up with a prosperous but hideous beast.
She tried to find something in him to admire,
But a fellow can't be ugly his whole life and not be affected
In an unseemly way. So one night at bedtime she placed
Her ring on the table and left, having learned the hard way
That many a monster has the shape of a man.

Three Sluggards

One

If I were asleep and smelled smoke,
I would not open my eyes
to see if the house were afire.

Two

If I were warming myself by that flame,
I would rather let my heel be burned
than to draw back my leg.

Three

If I were to be hanged for arson
and someone put a sharp knife in my hand,
I wouldn't bother to cut the rope.

Epilogue

The fame of the three spread far and wide,
even got them elected to office
where they caused little harm
as they idled their hours until pension-time.

"Greeting the Frog" by Walter Crane in *Walter Crane's Picture Books*, 1900.

The Frog King

for James H. Bowden

Iron Henry slept under
    the princess's pillow in a time
        when wishes still came true.

But acts of passion frequently disenchant,
    and there aren't many good strategies
        for sleeping with a woman

so full of narcissistic desire. It was hard
    to settle on the right word,
        but as she dreamt

Henry whispered endearments sweet enough
    to make stones cry. Words poured from his mouth
        as easily as water from a shoe.

And each morning he shook the eiderdown
    until its feathers fell like snow, and at last
        she undid the laces of her stay.

You can dismiss this as a miniature domestication myth
    or merely a tale about an amphibian intruder,
        but, even if she has to kiss a frog,

every princess hungers for Iron Henry in bed,
    and any old frog may one morning
        find a fat pillow beneath his head.

The Little Tailor and the Flies

The little tailor popped his head out the door
When he heard a woman hawking preserves.
He bought a quarter-pound and spread it on bread
Intending to eat it after he finished stitching a fine doublet.

While he sewed, flies gathered, rubbing their legs
As they walked across the ceiling. Eventually they swarmed
Upon the bread. Every time he brushed them away,
They returned. Angered, the tailor picked up a swath
Of cloth and brought it down fiercely. Seven flies lay dead
On the spot. They likely deserved killing, he thought,
But see how little liberties sometimes lead to great offenses.

The Boy Who Wanted To Learn What Fear Was

My elder brother was smart,
a wagoner who gave my father
no trouble.

Our bearded cousin
seined for gudgeon
in fresh water.

But no amount of toil can make me shudder;
he who wants to be a sickle
must first learn to bend.

I have seen the gallows where
they said I would marry
the ropemaker's daughter.

But that's where I thought
I would at last learn to fly.

A Better Bargain

A peasant drove his pig to the fair and sold her for seven talers.
On the way home he heard frogs crying *I'm broke! I'm broke!*
so he took the money from his pocket and counted it out
before them. The frogs paid no attention to his reckoning.
Count it yourselves then he said and threw the money into the water.
You pond-splashers, you thickheads, you goggle-eyes,
you have big mouths and can croak, but you cannot count.

Months later he took his cow to slaughter
and calculated that he might profit by selling its meat
and saving its hide. But on the way a pack of dogs
followed him to the butcher's door and began to bark
and sniff the meat. *I know you well, you curs, and whom you serve.*
I will leave this for you if you promise to bring me my money in three days.

The dogs fell upon the cow, but weeks passed
and no one came to pay. *There is no trusting anyone*
the peasant thought. Patience gone, he went to the butcher himself
and demanded payment. *I must have my money.*
Did not a big dog pay you for my slaughtered cow?

The butcher took his broomstick and drove out
the countryman who went to the palace
and begged for an audience. The king asked what injury
the man had suffered *Alas, the frogs and dogs have taken*
what is mine, and the butcher has paid me with a stick.

The king's daughter laughed so heartily
that the monarch said *I cannot give you justice,*
but you shall have my daughter who has never guffawed
so hard as she just did at you. Go into
my treasure chamber and get some coins for yourself.

He did not need to be told twice; he stuffed
whatever would fit into the pockets of his old coat,
then replied *no, I do not want your daughter at all.*
I have a wife, and she is one too many.
At home it is as if she stands in every corner.
The king grew angry and called him a no-good lout.

Ah, lord the peasant sighed *but what can you expect*
from an ox but beef? He went straight to the inn
and tallied his treasure. Then he wept.
I once knew what I had; then the world deceived me.
Now how can I tell if what's in my pockets is right?

"The Three Bears" by Arthur Rackham in *English Fairy Tales*, 1927.

Three Bears

While they waited for their breakfast porridge to cool,
A girl peered into the bears' keyhole and lifted the latch.
She sampled each dish and sat in all three canebottom chairs,
Then she entered the bedchamber where the bears had slept.

When the trio returned home, they saw the emptied bowls
And broken seats. In the next room the littlest bear found the girl,
A plump pillow beneath her blonde head. His shrill voice
Startled her awake: *someone is lying in my bed.*

Perhaps he was surprised because he was young and naïve;
He didn't know that people had been lying to one another
For a long time. So the girl opened the window and ran
Into the woods. As in a bad divorce, the family saw no more of her.

The Youngest Daughter

Beauty is forever the youngest daughter,
the one who believes her own footsteps,
but she is a tomb that opens from the inside.

Her love is always as far away as the sky is blue
and as short as a day of rain.
Gold coins fall whenever she speaks,

and some young dumbling,
blinded by briars and with blood in his shoes,
is always there to count them and pick them up.

Reliable as a bad meal after a funeral,
he would push a ghost down the stairs for her
or if necessary bowl with the skulls of priests.

But the simpleton who wins this bride
lies down on hard straw.
Wood shavings become his coffin pillow.

This is just how some love starts –
with an unwary heart – but ends
with every commandment broken.

Until the Leaves Tremble

suppose someone said
as you sat by his fire
roasting oxen on a spit
that you had killed three giants

perhaps he was a one-eyed captain
who also accused you of stealing
the king's daughter's shoe and then
he pulled a needle from his sleeve

and threatened to blind you
no matter what your lucky stars foretold
who knows what enchantments
or braveries might have made him as bold

as the crows in the cornfield
has he ever used the rib
of a gray whale for a spoon
or a canyon for a crib

would a man who kills giants
bring such a fool to harm
or would you let him babble in his beer
until his saliva was no longer warm

"Puss in Boots" in *Fairy Tales that Never Grow Old*.

Puss 'n Boots

A woodsman may leave uncut trees for his children,
but the miller had no legacy – just a rotting mill,
a sorry donkey, and a half-starved cat. When his estate
was divided, the eldest son took the mill, the second one
the ass, leaving for the youngest only the cat.

The older two might earn an honest living
from their inheritance, but the younger reasoned
that, if he ate the cat and sold the skin,
he would in short order surely perish.

The old tale would have you believe that
the cat, startled by those words, told him
 "Give me a pair of boots to trudge through
the thickets with, and you shall see I'm worth
more than you imagine." But he was particularly lazy
and not especially clever at catching mice,
nor was he eager to stalk through the thorns. Get real!
Only an oafish master would give him the boots he asked for.

Denied, the cat filled his bag with lettuce and bran and headed
to the rabbit warren where he lay barefoot aping the dead.
His scheme was to tempt young hares, ignorant of the world,
to enter the bag headlong by the prospect of an easy feast.
Then he would draw tight the string and dine. Days later
he was hungry again; in Plan B he hid in a cornfield
to lure partridges into the trap. The cat did well enough with his snares,
but he did not grow fat. And, being feline, he was not about
to share his success. So what was this business with the boots about?

The days of fairies and elves are gone. There are no
magic cloaks, flying chariots, or venomous swords,
but we too have our household deities. Today we live in a world full
of cats from whom in our vanity we continue to learn our own lessons.

"Chicken Little" by J. G. Chandler from *The Remarkable Story of Chicken Little*, 1840.

The Farmer's Chickens

the farmer told the chickens
to come in and enjoy the crumbs
from his table

they declined
knowing their mistress
would beat them if she found out

the farmer said she would not know
and pestered the birds
to come inside

they climbed onto the table
and dined all afternoon
until the woman returned

when they ran to get outside
she grabbed her broom
and beat them heartily

the next day they were invited
back to the table all roasted and divine
their young necks twisted and wrung

The Shoemaker

the shoemaker's old dog Sultan
had lost his teeth
and no thief was afraid
so he vowed that the next day
he would kill the hound

but the shoemaker had never learned
what dogs mean when they bark
and when Sultan did
a bird flew beyond the branch where
funereal jays had already gathered

the shoemaker looked at the bird
and called to his wife
its feathers are red and green
and shine like stars
oh, bird, sing me your song again

but no bricklebrit could bring it back
so be happy, friends, for your breadsop and potato
even if one day is like another
at least at night you have a pillow

Today Given, Tomorrow Sold

what would suit you
if you were poor

and slept on a bed of straw
behind the stove

or what if you wed
a beautiful woman

in a magnificent dress
one who had lost her way

but clad you
like a foreign lord

and kept her tongue
in a knapsack

would a woman
who picked your clothes

but not your lice
make you smile

"The Spider and the Fly" by Arthur Rackham from *Aesop's Fables*, 1912.

Thumb

a boy no bigger than the tip of his father's thumb
was tied to a thistle so he wouldn't blow away

at night he slept in a walnut shell
and bathed in a tiny bowl

in time the family cow took a fancy
to his oak-leaf hat and swallowed him like a pill

but she regurgitated him in her cud
and he lived to tell that tale

however Tom's days were numbered
a spider mistook him for a fly

and her poisonous breath killed him
on a leaf where he often stood

she sucked up his future along with
the last drop of his failing human blood

On the Other Hand

A middle-aged man courted two women:
one young, the other well advanced in years.
The elder, ashamed at being courted by a man
so much younger, pulled out black hairs
from his head every time he slept over.

The younger did not wish to be the wife
of an old man and zealously pulled out
every grey hair she could find.

Made bald by both, in time
he found himself balled by neither.

The Giant Killer

The first giant died when he toppled
from his terrace into a pit that Jack
had dug with his pickaxe and shovel.

The second, Old Blunderbore, vowed
to feast upon Jack's flesh.
But like a Bond villain, the giant had lost
his way and revenge became his compass.

Though you lodge in your own bed tonight,
you shall not see the morning light,
the giant vowed when he came for him.
But in Jack's bed the giant found a billet of wood instead
which he broke as easily as he would have the boy's bones.

Beckett knew you didn't have to be hunted
to hide, but, when you find out what the big boys
are up to, be prepared to run. And do not expect
to escape injury for the pain you caused,
even when done to a deserving oaf.
No argument can give courage to a coward.

The Hatchlings

Three young ones sat in a swallow's nest.
When they fledged, they flew away
on a high wind and lighted in a wheatfield

where a million others had assembled.
*Let's go back to the garden and feed
on caterpillars and worms*

until the cherries are ripe the oldest said. Ah, son,
spoke the father, such tidbits are not bad, but there
is great risk. People in gardens often carry long poles.

I'll go to court then the second said. *There
I'll dwell amid gold, velvet, armor, and fine robes.*
No, you must keep to the horses' stable

where they winnow oats, the father warned.
That's where fortune gives you your daily corn.
Yes the second agreed. Little birds

encounter great dangers, and, when stable-boys
make traps and fix their gins and snares
in the straw, many a one gets caught.

But if you go to court, the old bird said,
and leave no feathers, you have learned a great deal
indeed about how to go about in the world.

Always look around you and above,
for wolves often devour even the wisest dogs.
The father then questioned the third.

Where will you seek your fortune? he asked.
Along the cart-roads and highways
where I'll beg for barley and corn.

Keep with your own kind the father cautioned.
Feed on spiders and moths from the trees.
Then may you live in peace.

The world, it seems, is full of wicked birds
with crooked beaks and long claws,
ones that lie in wait for smaller prey.

Nothing falls to the ground except by God's will,
and whoever feeds himself without injuring others
fares well. Take refuge in churches if you must

and keep the buzzing flies away,
but remember that the Lord above hears
the cries of ravens too,

and he who commits himself to His ways
will not be fooled that all is well.
Even if the world were empty,

sparrows would still suffer and weep
while malicious birds pray over their bones.
So sleep with an eye open . . . and always watch for stones.

"Sleeping Beauty" by C.M. Burd, 1919.

Prince Charming Breaks His Silence

wicked girls can be nice morsels
fat as young quails fit for devouring
despite their spiteful ways

enchanted they'll sometimes sleep a hundred years
lapdogs beside them in their splendid beds
a dozen musicians dozing nearby

when at last I married one
we had sex for breakfast for a month
then the spits quit turning and all the fires went out

The Test

"Go," the old hag said
And bring back three hairs
From the Devil's head.

So the challenge lay at his feet,
One that smacked of sure defeat.

After closer thought he stroked his chin.
"I tell you now what I told you before,
I never want to see my ex-wife again."

Three Fables, One Moral

A wolf had a bone in his throat and hired
a crane for a large sum to remove it.
When the bird demanded payment, the wolf
grinned and ground his teeth: your recompense is
having withdrawn your head from the jaws of a wolf.

A second wolf encased himself in the skin
of a sheep and pastured with the flock.
In the evening he was shut in the fold
by the shepherd who came later that night
to secure food for the morrow's meal.
Instead of a sheep, he slit the wolf's throat.

A grasshopper shivering from famine
begged for food from a tribe of ants.
Why did you not treasure up food
during the summer? they asked.
I passed the day singing, he replied.
To which they answered: If you were
foolish enough to sing all summer,
you shall dance supperless this winter.

Calamity tests the sincerity of friends.
The price for getting what we wish
is often someone else's ruination.
He is wisest who is warned
by the misfortune of others.

"The Poisoned Princess" by J. Moyr Smith in *The Old Fairy Tales*, 1876.

A Rose by Another Name

In the morning the dwarfs went into the mountains
To dig for iron and gold, then came home ready for supper
Only to find Snow lying breathless on the floor.
They did everything they could to bring her back to life,
But nothing worked, so they laid her on a bier and mourned
Three long days. They would have buried her too, but she
Looked lifelike, and her cheeks were still rosy.

So they built a glass coffin and laid her in it atop a mountain
Where she lay for many years unchanged, dumb as a fish,
In a gown sewn of stitchweed until a prince found her.
They celebrated their wedding with much pomp, but often
 in marriage a woman changes nothing but the name of her master.

Little Brother

Little brother said: we have no happiness.
Mother is dead, and our step-mother beats us every day.
When we come near, she kicks us away.
Even the little dog under our table
feeds on hard crust. God pity us.

So the two went into the world
walking fields, meadows, and stony places;
none was under God's good graces,
and it was hardgoing for the girl

who thought the rain was heaven weeping.
They sobbed together that evening and collapsed,
wearied by sorrow and hunger from the miles elapsed,
and lay in a hollow tree.

When they awoke, the sun was high and shone
upon them. Then the sister said *I am hot with thirst*.
But the step-mother had bewitched the forest,
and their throats were as dry as a butcher's bone.

So when they found falling water
leaping lightly over rocks, she bent to drink.
Then the sister heard the water speak
as if it were the voice of God's own daughter.

It said *whoever drinks of me will be a deer*.
And when the brother drank from his palm,
he fell asleep. He was so calm
that around his collar she tied her garter;

then she plucked rushes and braided them
into a cord and led him deeper into the wood.
When they came to a little house, things were good,
she thought; *I can stay here forever with him.*

Then she fed her roe-brother tender grass from her hand,
and she gathered roots and berries, piped a tune.
But there would be worse misfortune:
when he heard the huntsmen's bugle, he ran.

Turnips Below Ground, Corn Above

Turnips below ground, corn
and blooming buckwheat above,
the weasel stood by his door
enjoying the morning breeze.
He sipped from his bottle of brandy
and sang the song he sang every day.

He never suspected that a jughound
was yearning to cut him from throat to lap,
sew a coat according to his skin,
and cover his own bald head with a cap.

Three Travelers

Three travelers came upon an ant-hill.
Two wanted to destroy it, to see the pests flee
and carry their eggs away in terror,
but the other, a simpleton,
said *let them live in peace.*

Then they came to a lake on which a great number
of ducks swam. Two wanted
to catch a couple for roasting, but the other
would not permit it. *I will not suffer
you to kill them and forever be haunted.*

In time they came to a hive whose honey
overflowed down the trunk of a tree.
Two wanted to make a fire and suffocate
the honeymakers, but the third said
I cannot allow you to burn them, the bees.

You needn't guess – that night they dined
on feathers and dumplings of stone
while near them little rabbits
ate cabbage until at last the sensible pair
killed the third and went on alone.

The Prince's Wingmen

The fat man lay like a bale of hay beside the road.
When the prince passed, he called out:
Take me into service. Though I am podgy,
I can make myself a thousand times stouter.

After a while they found a man lying
with his ear to the ground. What are you doing?
the king's son asked. *Listening* he replied.
Nothing escapes my ears; I can even hear the grass grow.

Tell me then, sir, what you hear at the court
of the old queen with the beautiful daughter.
I hear the whizzing of a sword striking off a wooer's head.

The trio walked on until they saw a pair
of legs and feet. Some distance beyond
they came to the torso and at last to the head.

Oh, I'm a tall rascal alright, but, when I really stretch out,
I'm a thousand times taller than the highest mountain.
I will gladly walk with you if you will take me along.

Then they found a man with bandaged eyes;
whatever he looked at split into pieces.

When the five reached the queen's court,
she was delighted to have snared so many in her net.
She said I will give you three tasks, and, if you perform them all,
you shall remain free. Three hundred fat oxen are feeding
in the meadow behind my palace. These you must eat –
skin, hair, bones, and horn. Below in my cellar lie
three hundred casks of wine; these you must drink.
If one hair or drop remains, your lives are forfeit to me.

The fat man puffed himself and ate the oxen.
Is this all I am to have for breakfast? he asked.
Then he drank the wine straight from the casks,
drained them to the dregs without carafe or glass.

Next came the queen's second task:
fetch me the ring I dropped into the sea.
So the man with sharp sight said
I will split the ocean and see where it lies.
When he did, the fat man drank
the water, and the tall man reached
down and brought up the band.

You shall not escape with your heads.
This night I will bring my daughter
to your chamber, prince, and you shall
enfold her, but, when twelve strikes,
if she is not in your arms, you are lost.

The prince thought it would be easy to keep
his arms wrapped around such a beautiful girl,
but he knew that treachery lurked.
Keep watch he told the men and make sure
the maiden does not leave my room.

When the young woman surrendered herself
to the prince, the tall one wound himself
around the couple, and the stout one placed himself
against the door. The moon shone brightly
through the window onto the damsel's face.
But at eleven the queen cast such a spell
that all of them fell asleep and the girl was carried away.

The men slept soundly until a quarter of
when the magic lost its power and all awoke again.
The prince's servants began to lament,
but the listener said *Be quiet so I can hear.*
He listened for a moment and said *She is on a rock
three hundred leagues away bewailing her fate.
If you hurry, tall one, you will need only a few steps.*

He reached her quickly, and they were back by twelve,
merry and happy and almost in love. Then the aged sorceress
came stealing, believing her daughter was still
on the rock. But when she saw her, she was alarmed.
She fussed awhile. Then the fat man spat a time
or two; the expelled sea-water caused a great lake
to rise – then it drowned the whole crew.

One Father's Trick

Sons, there is great treasure hidden in my vineyards,
the old farmer said on his deathbed.

So after he passed, they took their spades
and mattocks and dug up every portion
of the land but found no treasure.

The vines, however, luxuriated
and repaid their efforts.

The old man knew it is the consciousness
of our predicament not the soil
that makes our wine taste bitter.

"Hansel and Gretel" by Arthur Rackham in *Grimm's Fairy Tales*, 1909.

Fairy Tale

In the oldest ones carpentry is confection,
the curtains candy with a licorice braid
though the roof eavesdrop like an old crone
covered with the excrement of paltry birds.
The furniture is familiar, the sort men
might make were their hands tames flesh
or their childfeet not turned to hoof:
To be enchanted is to live in a house of cake.

The moon, cleaner than a picked bone,
shines through trees where hatchjawed ravens sit.

It is a dream like children have, the one
of home before they gain their wits
and Mother calls from the kitchen
where the sweetbreads cool.
Lured and obedient, they come to her stunned
like trancewalkers beneath the curse
dreaming their first taste of lust
and ready like Hansel to enter the oven.

A Game of Chicken

Two gamecocks fought for mastery of the henyard
until one at last put the other to flight.
The lesser skulked in a quiet corner.

His conqueror flew atop a high wall where
he flapped his wings and crowed with all his might.
An eagle then soared by and carried him out of sight,
leaving the vanquished bird to rule without dispute.
Evil wishes – like chickens – generally come home to roost.

Donkey, Dog, Cat, and Ram

we are all sons of sorrow
eating from a wooden bowl

the goat in the churchyard
not much different
from the dancer in the graveyard

still silence can be redemptive
though it's better not to be too human than
to find emotional equity only in ourselves

we'll live with the smutch of elfinkind
until we're turned into birds, are slaughtered
or the donkey one day spits gold

About the Author

Jerry Bradley, a member of the Texas Institute of Letters, is University Professor of English and the Leland Best Distinguished Faculty Fellow at Lamar University. He won the 2017 Boswell Poetry Prize awarded by Texas Christian University and in 2018 received writing awards from the Conference of College Teachers of English and the Texas College English Association. He is the author of ten books including five previous full-length poetry collections: *Simple Versions of Disaster* (University of North Texas Press), *The Importance of Elsewhere* (Ink Brush Press), *Crownfeathers and Effigies* (Lamar University Literary Press), *South of the Boredom* (Angelina River Press), and *Collapsing into Possibility* (Lamar University Literary Press).

Bradley's poems have appeared in *New England Review*, *American Literary Review*, *Modern Poetry Studies*, and *Southern Humanities Review*. He is the long-time poetry editor of *Concho River Review*. He is also a past-president of the Texas Association of Creative Writing Teachers, the Conference of College Teachers of English, and the Southwest Popular and American Culture Association which endows a writing award in his name.

In 2014 Bradley was named a Piper Professor, an award that annually recognizes ten top Texas professors. In 2000 he received the Joe D. Thomas Scholar-Teacher of the Year from the Texas College English Association and the 2005 Frances Hernandez Teacher-Scholar Award from the Conference of College Teachers of English. He was named Outstanding Alumnus from Midwestern State University's College of Liberal Arts in 2002.

More information is available on his Wikipedia page (Jerry Bradley, poet) and personal website: www.jerrybradley.net. He may be contacted at jerry.bradley@lamar.edu

www.ingramcontent.com/pod-product-compliance
Lightning Source LLC
Chambersburg PA
CBHW040323050426
42453CB00018B/2443